David Corfe

The Road Taken

Selected Poems, 1990-2013

Preface by the Right Reverend John B. Taylor

The Road Taken

David Corfe

Geoff.

With much gratitude,

David

Published in 2014 by FeedARead Publishing
Copyright © David Corfe.

British Library C.I.P.

A CIP catalogue record for this title is available from the British
Library

For my wife, Rosemary, and all our family

Acknowledgements

With much gratitude to Geoffrey Daniel, of the Association of Christian Writers, for his very helpful critique and encouragement, and to Brendan McCusker and the Romsey poetry group for getting me started again.

Special thanks; to John Taylor, from whom I learnt to appreciate the Old Testament, at Oakhill in 1968.

Highfield Church homegroup for their practical support and encouragement, and to John Morrison for designing the cover.

The Foreshore, Lepe, page 21, and 9/11, page 45, appeared in the Southern Daily Echo in 2001. The Subaltern's Lament, page 7, was published in the New Forest Park Culture magazine in April 2013.

Preface

Here is a collection of 60 short pieces of poetry composed and compiled over a period of twenty years or more. The uniting feature is that it is largely autobiographical, from the hand of a former missionary finding his way in India and later to become an established clergyman in a range of ministries from London to Manchester.

Any parson writing about himself cannot spare himself his occasional failures and doubts, but equally he cannot hide his strong faith and evangelical leanings. Corfe writes movingly about his visits to the homes of people of other faiths and equally about his certainties over Christ's sufferings and death on the Cross.

Any poet who writes at all Christianly is vulnerable to the twin criticisms of cringe or banality. I can find none of this. Indeed every piece comes over with verbal beauty and precision. There is so much to admire, whether in the amusing variant on Miss Joan Hunter Dunn, or observing the birds on the tit-feeder in his garden or (supremely) in the poem on the Word made Flesh.

I wish we could have more like this, much more. Has David Corfe no more in his knapsack to inspire his grateful readership? I have rarely discovered anything to match his brilliance with words and ideas.

The Right Reverend J .B Taylor. Former Bishop of St. Alban's.

Contents

The Road Mistaken?

after Robert Frost

So many paths diverged in the wood
I was bemused; I couldn't guess
how each would twist from where I stood
or reach to where I thought I should
be going. The choice seemed limitless.

I took, I thought, the straightest track,
the steepest, what seemed most direct,
but as I climbed I tired, grew slack,
admired the paths behind my back;
was my chosen route correct?

From high above the woods I saw
tracks below now lost in shade.
The richness of the valley floor
attracted me Should I explore —
reverse the youthful choice I'd made?

Ah, but above and out of view
mountains surely waited, tall
and sharp against the sky, and blue,
with dazzling snows. I must renew
my journey upwards, risking all.

1

Wordy Journey

I've often travelled in the realms of words —
delighted in a few of Shakespeare's speeches
and followed Wordsworth on his fells. I've heard
the tide of faith recede on *Dover Beach,*
surveyed the *Waste Land's* broken images.
The pity and futility of war
I learned through Owen; in the early stages
of my journey willingly absorbed,
or feigned, a mood of disillusionment —
the world was so much with me. Yet behind
the *Hound of Heaven* never would relent
in his pursuit. I fled him down my mind
until he caught me. Willingly I ask
him now to batter my heart, complete his task.

The Curate

This outfit isn't me. Dark suit or cassock,
collar shiny white, reversed, I'm set
apart to be a shepherd of your flock
and labelled "holy", but I'm conscious yet
how much of me refuses to conform.
I want to get it right, I'd like to speak
profound and penetrating truths to warm
your frozen people, but know my faith is weak,
I doubt the very things I teach. Should I
continue to sustain this act, and search
for inner peace — or is it all a lie
to be renounced, and with it, perhaps, the church?
Dear God, I can't go struggling on alone;
will you forever be my great unknown?

Aesthete in a Warm Climate

Thank you, Lord, that I am not at all
like other tourists; don't follow in the flock
behind a guide, or, coach-bound, crawl
in traffic to view it through tinted glass. Baroque
and Gothic, Art Nouveau, no artist's skill
is lost on me; I challenge guides with insight,
and avoid the bawdy nightlife. Yet still
I'm troubled. Lord, the girls you've made excite
more than a passing glance; your sun's hot,
they wear so little. My heart is beating faster
amongst these Botticelli forms; I'm not
so very old or past it. Dearest Master,
they're beautiful. You'll have to hold me tight,
teach me true love, and help me guard my sight.

Rembrandt Self-Portrait

You couldn't count the hours I've watched this face,
studied its wrinkled contours, gazed within
the eyes reflected to meet mine, traced
the record of my life beneath the skin.

I'm glad I've left behind vainglorious youth,
flamboyant gesture and exotic dress;
my fading smock serves well to tell the truth,
the slanting light catches its warm darkness.

The curls have greyed beneath my ancient cap,
so too the whiskers on my lip and chin;
my skin is mottled like a well-thumbed map,
the veins show through in placcs where it's thin.

As for my nose, that bulbous knob that thrusts
at me so strongly, I have to mix grit
with the paint to get its texture. Age encrusts
each feature as I faithfully record it.

Groan as I may, yet let me not despair;
thank God I still have eyes as keen as new.
A pattern of decay confronts my stare,
but I shall paint God's image breaking through.

In a National Trust Tea Shop

They found each other on the internet,
both grey and middle-aged, but hopeful yet.
Becalmed amid the café's noisy sea
they sat, she with averted eyes, while he
held her hand and stroked her fingers. Her face
was flushed and shone, she fumbled with her necklace.
He thought she signalled that her heart now longed
like his for friendship, love, and to belong.
She wanted to surrender, but in her mind
her adult family cried out behind
to tell her she was mad. Long in silence
they were poised, he eager, she with the sense
it was too late. They watched the wan sun set
lost in dreams and unexpressed regret.

A Subaltern's Lament

With thanks to John Betjeman

Joan Hunter Dunn, my Joan Hunter Dunn,
the years have passed by, so much left undone
since we played our first tournament, followed by gin,
and in your old Hillman that memorable spin.

We've followed your hearse by woodland ways
redolent still of that late summer haze;
but blind are your eyes to the westering sun,
earth thuds on your coffin-lid, Joan Hunter Dunn.

And secretly now I admit to the truth
that my passion for you passed away with my youth;
for when once you became my obedient wife
you tried to control every part of my life.

I came to detest the chime of your voice
and your tennis-girl's hand; regretted my choice
under the intimate roof of your car,
where you trapped me, so artlessly artful you are.

I stuck with you faithfully, more or less, Joan,
tried to maintain a gentleman's tone;
but now that you're buried I plan to have fun,
my plain Mrs Smith, née Joan Hunter Dunn.

Rosie

(exhibited at the Royal Society of British Artists,
1967)

She stares through half-closed eyes beneath a fringe
and pulls at a purple stocking, almost naked,
propped on a tousled bed. After forty years
her thin limbs are still immune to cold.
What did my father feel when painting her,
this young flesh arranged for their evening study,
a girl forever caught in the act of dressing?

Life classes weren't for me — the sagging forms,
objective tracing of the curves of breasts,
glances between the thighs. And when a model
caught my eye in hers I was unnerved.
Perhaps old Adam felt like me when first
he fell, shame spoilt his innocence,
and both grabbed frantically for fig-leaves?
Alas, I know Old Adam all too well.

Dissonance

Lithe, swiftly as a deer she goes,
with auburn mane, attractive to the eyes.
Her 'cello sings exquisitely, it flows
with passion, dances, meditates and sighs.

We didn't know her well when she first came
asking for lodgings — it was a business deal.
But day by day her hoarded food laid claim
to half our fridge, and overflowed to steal
space in the cupboards. If she could eat it all,
or when, she never told us. Locked behind
the bathroom door alone she was in thrall
to a powerful sickness of the mind.

A life of beauty chained by such compulsion —
Lord, rescue her, and me from my revulsion

Eve

It was her joy to serve, but now all day
she sits propped in a chair, again a baby.
What can she understand? Her eyes betray
no flicker of emotion, creeping bodily
decay her only future. Can she still
pace inside her prison walls and test
the locks? Will she grieve in secret till
she falls embittered to her final rest?
Her carers may be tempted soon to choose,
for love, a painless route for her, a clinic,
to preserve some dignity, reduce
the watching. Is there hope for one so sick?
This only, that the Lord of life knows best,
and in her ruined prison is her guest.

A Touch of Healing

Her life was leaking; shamed by a bloody trail
she was unclean, cut off from God and friends,
her savings spent on quacks, to no avail.
Then comes this man, whose power they say extends to
heal, to her own village. She expends
her failing strength, ignores the shame, to thrust
towards him, stoop, and touch his hem in trust.

Transfusion surges through her, energy
that heals her womb. Amazed she tries to fall
again unseen into the crowd, while he,
despite the press, stops and turns to call,
"Who touched me?" Fearfully she tells him all,
and in the telling finds her shame now ceases;
she sings for joy, with all whom Christ releases.

The Samaritan at the Well

I went at noon to fill my bucket, and there
he was, a Jew, sitting by our well
asking for a drink; he didn't shrink
from a defiled female and her cup.

I was slow to understand; thought
he spoke of a better well, a cleaner spring.
Though even then I felt a thirst growing
for love, different from my love for men.

He knew all about me, like a prophet;
that was painful. I changed the subject,
talked about Messiah coming to explain.
He took my breath away, said it was him.

I knew it was true. Love came pouring in
through him, clean, fresher than any well.
I couldn't keep it in, I had to tell,
and go on telling.

Mary at Bethany

Your words to me are water in a desert —
would that I might sit here all my days,
my Lord, my friend, my love, my hope, my power;
power to raise my brother four days dead
when we despaired, waiting, it seemed in vain —
see now how he sits with us at table.

What can I give you? This precious flask must do;
my happiness is at your calloused feet
as eagerly I break its narrow neck,
control my trembling and pour it all out,
empty the flask of my overflowing heart.

Be pleased to enjoy the fragrance at your feet
and as it fills the room — it's all I have.
Let others claim my love is wasteful Lord,
if only I may kneel here in silence.

The Centurion's Story

As we drove nails
through his flesh
we heard him gasping
forgiveness.

We did a
a painstaking job,
his hands and feet were
well bloodied.

Thirty three,
we cut him short;
he seemed to think his
work complete.

Did he doubt?
We heard him cry,
then entrust himself
to his God.

Could it be
that to pardon
all us murderers
he gave blood?

When we killed
him did he think
he was some sort of
sacrifice?

His empty
tomb challenged us;
we guessed death at last
was done for.

Word Made Flesh

The fleshliness of God — behold this baby
nuzzling at the breast, whose minute hands
feel for its intimate warmth, close on a finger.
Nappies smelling of digested milk,
arms uncoordinated, legs-a-kick,
a language of cries and tears, faint smiles
and the gentle breathing of innocent sleep;
God opening his heart to man.

Stand below this bloody post, look,
if you can, at his contorted face and form
spread-eagled on the wood. Hear him gasp,
heave upwards on the nails struggling for breath
twist as muscles knot and nerves burn.
Hear him pray for his captors and the crowd
as we wait helplessly below. This is
God, with punctured side, stabbed to the heart.

Now come in the early dawn to the tomb's mouth.
The dead weight of stone has rolled, the shroud
that bound is empty and collapsed; gone
the battered corpse; transformed he meets his friends.
Listen for his invitation, steady
your hand to feel the scars, reach
the very heart of God revealed in flesh —
and fall before his majesty and grace.

Psalm for Spring

Maytime on the Downs. Buzzards circle above,
breasting the currents with precision,
while larks on eager wings press upwards singing;
they drop bubbles of rounded sound
from invisible heights of blue.
I plod the rough track fumbling for words
of gratitude to the Creator.

Clouds push shadows across fields
where young wheat rustles and rape in strident yellow
dominates the air with scent.
Hedgerows foam white froth of hawthorn and cow-
                                   parsley
above tangles of sappy green —
astonishing abundance
of never ceasing workmanship.

Beyond earshot and the hill
the distant town must toil and bustle,
aware only that the sun today is warm.
I turn towards it grateful for the music of the Downs
still singing in my memory;
I shall try with greater faithfulness to use
the voice my God has given me.

Autumn

It warms its hands by
a dying fire; life shelters
under tawny blankets.

At the window-panes
a frantic daddy-long-legs
reaches for the sun.

Leaf solar panels,
fused by excess of summer,
burn red and yellow.

Mists veil the meadows;
in the woods fleshy toadstools
erupt and decay.

Invisible grubs
make compost and prepare for
a spring resurrection.

Southampton Common

These ancient oak-trees cut me down to size,
a little ant that crawls about their base;
their warts and furrows hint at memories
of ages long before my coming to this place.
They saw an army camped, equipped for France,
and sheltered fugitives in Civil War,
saw public hangings, and still give a glance
to lovers tangling on their root-rough floor.
And I am small, as transient as the breeze
which stirs and sighs through these arthritic boughs;
I shall be felled, I fear, before the trees —
though not before the Lord of time allows.
He holds me, like an acorn, in his hand,
to die and rise renewed at his command.

II

I seemed to drown in other creatures' joy —
touched a new world inside the shady wood,
though feared my clumsy presence might destroy
the lilting music of the birds I could
not see, their joyful counterpoint. I stood
entranced, a dumb intruder on this throng
who sang as if they never ever should
cease pouring out their bubbling stream of song;
a powerful instinct seemed to make them long
to join in praise. In a world so sad,
so mangled by man's selfishness and wrong,
they sang in innocence, and I was glad.
What then? I'll sonnet with them and rejoice
in Him who gave each one their special voice.

Landscape with Figures

Old Winchester Hill

The air was crisp as winter's grip gave way.
Puffy clouds took time to saunter white
across intensities of blue, while rays
of sun kindled shifting pools of light.
Above a buzzard slowly circled round
his chosen acreage of field and tree,
while on the chalky hill-top a rough mound
of workings long predated history.
We tottered on the pathway, you and I,
feeling the joys and weight of seventy springs,
small beneath the great expanse of sky;
gazed and exclaimed, each seeing different things.
And He was there, our landscape-loving God,
who knew the stones of every path we trod.

The Foreshore, Lepe

Step beyond the car park where the trees
run down to the shingle, and the mud shines bright
as a mirror, polished by the restless seas.
Hear the gulls cry and dive and fight,
see the waders patter, beaks probing the weed.
Roses bloom, luminous and pale,
gorse-pods explode, scattering seed.

Only the concrete tells another tale —
how this wrecked platform echoed to the sound
of dreadful preparation. In secret here
were quays and towers and gun emplacements bound
for France, a floating port and all its gear;
while all the length of this defiant shore
millions of men stood ready, poised for war.

*Part of the Mulberry Harbour was assembled and
launched at Lepe before the invasion of Normandy in
1944*

The Rising Sun, Warsash

The windows of the "Rising Sun"
beckon through fog. It's damp,
and all is washed to chilly grey,
the river, sky and trees.

Gold and bronze of falling leaves
are dulled, their fire extinguished;
the flames of the refining plant
are hidden in mist.

Heavy silence grips the river
sliding so gently;
a lone squadron of geese
wings in formation southwards.

On the quay fading wreathes
of poppies surround a stone
which marks the place where once commandos
embarked at night for France.

Boats were locked then side by side
jammed across the water,
as sweaty men, who hid their fear,
joked and checked their weapons,

laughed, and glimpsed each others' faces
lighting cigarettes;
then the roar of heavy engines
bore them into darkness.

In the bloody fog of conflict
they achieved their goal.
But fewer returned ever again
to watch the sun arising.

Warsash was one of many ports on the south coast from which units embarked for the invasion of Normandy.

A31, New Forest

The horses barely shift;
with leathery mouths they chew the gorse
while streams ruminate on pebbles;
the pines are still.

The whirr of cars and lorries
troubles the forest heart,
rubber hammering macadam,
men and women forever chasing time.

I dream of a national day of silence
as I settle and start my car
to add my extra decibels.
Let's switch off engines and ground planes,
be quiet.
We might then hear the ticking of our hearts
and face our inner restlessness.

Hide-Away Code

Shut inside his car
anonymous in armour
the mildest man
perhaps
just sometimes
puts his foot down and goes for it.
The thing becomes a tank
firing aggression.

Bird Feeding

Finches, tits, nuthatch, dunnock,
how hungrily they feed,
dart, flutter, perch, peck,
spill my precious seed.
Have they any thought, I wonder,
what it costs to meet their need,
who neither sow nor reap nor gather
into barns or plastic bags?

Pecking Order

Feeders for birds in a garden border
hung from a metal pole —
peanuts and fat, and a tube of seeds
with a perch by every hole.
And at dawn the birds began to eat,
they ate till the setting sun,
they pecked in an order they each understood
till the seed in the tube was done.

"Move over" said the great tit
as he hovered by the food;
"to sit there scoffing all day long
is very very rude."
And with a flurry and a flutter
of tiny whirring wings
he pushed a blue tit off her perch
despite her twittering.

A noisy gang of finches soon
descended on the seed.
"You tits have been here long enough
to satisfy your greed."
The finches then, in green and gold,
at once began to squabble;
the green ones teased and shoved the gold
till from their perch they wobbled.

A woodpecker in black and white,
splashed with brilliant red,
came flying from the nearby park
hoping he might be fed.
His beak was long and pointed,
he drilled the ball of fat;
the smaller birds all fled in fear —
they didn't stop to chat.

A squirrel with a tail that twitched
suddenly leapt from a tree,
and balanced on the pole's thin top
with practiced accuracy.
The pole swayed wildly from its weight,
the squirrel reached for the seed,
he hung upside-down as he clung to the tube,
desperate for a feed.

At that the patio door swung wide
and gramps came rushing out.
"You little thief". He clapped his hands,
hurling a stone with a shout.
The squirrel flicked his bushy tail
and vanished up a bough;
the feeder for birds stood all alone —
no one was feeding now.

To a Supermarket Trolley

Yes, I enjoy my trolley. In the grey company
of men who trail their women through the stores
my trolley is my joy — from the first fine
careless rapture as it responds lightly
to the touch, to my slow smooth pace behind
a heavy-laden cargo ship.

I hover discretely, waiting for the off.
My navigation skills are tested and
displayed with subtlety amidst the crowds;
we glide through narrow gaps, missing
the cans by millimeters, suddenly perform
amazing turns in vacant motorways,
relish mad moments with both hands
completely off the trolley.

Faces are firmly set, intent on lists
and prices, hunting perfect specimens
of fruit and veg., exotics from foreign climes,
unique offers to do ourselves some good.
I think of those toiling in the sun
for tea, coffee and bananas;
Their sweat congeals in my trolley.

Docking beside the check-out we repack,
pay customs dues, and slither sideways down
a ramp on to the car park. We unload
our wire container-ship; with final clash
it joins the other empties. We drive home,
ready to begin another week's consumption.

Spider

You hang in a corner.
Your spindle legs, octopus tentacles,
fan from a button-body central control.
You wait for your net of delicate threads
to jerk as flies are trapped.
You suck blood.
You're watching me now.

My duty today is dusting,
to eliminate webs.
I reason, summon my courage;
you're small, could you hurt me?
My duster is poised, spread on my hand;
please don't touch me.

There, see how lightly I have you folded —
no pain in that,
and here is the open window;
you will enjoy the garden,
let me shake you onto the lawn.

Oh, you're on the ledge outside
sorting your tangled legs.
You can't stay there,
I must shove you off.

But I have to confess
I feel ashamed;
I'm scared of you.
And why should I deprive you
of legitimate hunting,
especially when
I don't like flies?

The Lie

The stable was dark,
but the small room behind the sacking door
was darker still, its smell pungent.
We could just discern the ferret in its cage
crouching, sensing danger.
Fools, we made our dog attack it.
The cage gave way
and as the ferret bolted for freedom
the dog's teeth sank in its neck,
shaking till it was dead.
We staggered into the dazzling sunlight,
two murderers leaving a corpse.
And when the stable-man
asked about his animal
the lies we told
were darker in our hearts
than that small room
behind the sacking door.

Compost Revelation

I lifted the plastic from the heap
and stared at the foreign world below,
the scurrying woodlice, centipedes and earwigs,
twisting worms and slugs,
guessed at the million microbes working
with one united purpose
to turn these kitchen peelings
to fertile compost.
I gazed through the eyes of God
and saw that it was good,
how He delighted in each creature there,
knew them inside, their inner urgency,
enjoyed their bustling life.
Suddenly I knew myself at one,
one with my alien brothers,
one beneath the wide sky,
all together born
of the fecund imaginings of God.

Water-Lily

Roots probe the slime,
leaves ride the ripples.
She presses to the sun,
flexes wide her petals
in joyful self-exposure;
doesn't think of mud
or contemplate her beauty
when above there shines
light and energy and love.

The Bee

As lost bees beat themselves in vain
against a glass, frantic to reach the sun,
so we may beat ourselves in search of God.
His light streams through to stir and burn
but some transparent pane frustrates and stops us.
We have no peace, no, not until
we find the glass was shattered once by One
whose arms were deeply bloodied in the splintering;
He longs to lift us safely through the shards
and grant the access we desire.

Encountering Allah

This grey northern town seemed distant as Delhi
the shops which filled the pavements with exotic
fruits, the halal stalls and smells of incense,
the dark burquas which flitted and concealed
all but a woman's ankles, the splash of saris;
I was the foreigner.

I prayed on visiting my first imam,
the man who led the mosque; I feared Islam.
Would he receive a white evangelist?
Timidly I knocked his door, and he emerged
skull-cap askew, richly bearded, swarthy,
twinkling behind thick lenses.

He took my hand, welcomed me in, speaking
fluent English; his wife brought tea. The room
was full of papers, books, Korans and commentaries,
a child's plane hung from the ceiling. We sat
as he told his story; born in Africa
he had studied in Gujerat.

"Why? I wouldn't fight in another's war,
Zimbabwe's independence; I fled to India —
or Allah led me — to study the truths of Islam.
My studies led to being an imam."
He smiled as he thought of the subtle ways of God
who brought him to England.

I felt a growing oneness with this man,
his thirst for God and daily faithfulness.
"Allah is inscrutable," he said.
"He knows all I have done, is merciful,
but no, would never ever become a man,
as you suggest, to meet or knock my door."

We parted friends.

Aamir

I was sorry for Aamir, living alone
in a rented room at the top of a house,
with a wife somewhere in Pakistan
seeming unwilling to join him.

He shambled among tatty books —
a mixed collection of library seconds —
a few cracked plates, pots and bottles,
and brewed me sugary tea.

"In Pakistan I taught English lit.,
I struggled with Ulysees. Now hear
this Urdu gazal." He sighed and read,
savoured its fragrance.

He distanced himself from the brotherhood
of Islam, keeping a few old trusted
friends, but cherished freedom of thought;
was cautious of extremes.

"I often gaze from my window," he said,
"but fear to step outside; I'm like
a hunter who cleans his gun, then when
the lion roars — I run."

He came one year to our Christmas lunch
and winked as he drank the wine. He knew
what Christmas means, but feared to be seen
by a lion outside on the street.

Aziz

I knocked on a dozen doors through rainy streets;
shut or busy, why should they welcome me,
a white and wet evangelist? Turning
home I knocked on just one more, someone's
I hardly knew. Through a crack in the door —
"Aziz — you haven't heard? He died this morning."
The door swung wide and I was gently welcomed
into a darkened hall. I feared to intrude
on another's grief, unsure of etiquette,
took off my shoes and sidled to a place among
a group of men still as a stone-circle
on the floor, becapped, bearded and solemn.
Womens' voices drifted from the kitchen
and noise of children playing somewhere behind.
Aziz, the good man who had helped so many,
even Hindus in their need, was dead.
Thus we sat together, men of two
continents, together facing death.
Silence— no place to bandy rival doctrines,
though I thought I came at Christ's command;
He must have led me in my wanderings
in the rain and prompted the open door.
And now He sat where we sat in the silence
remembering Aziz.

Cry God for England and Saint George's

Our breath is foggy as we sing the hymns,
enjoy the cadences of good King James
and our dear Rector lovingly declaims
Cranmer's sonorous prayers. No modern whims
trouble our worship.

The mellow walls proclaim with pride our dead
who fought for empire — Omdurman, Khartoum,
Bengal, Punjab, inscriptions lost in gloom,
their regimental colours overhead
reminders of sacrifice.

A pale white Christ hangs stiffly in a pane
of our east window, but we can't forget,
glimpsed through another glass, a minaret
(funded by the Council once again)
to distract our worship.

What do they think they're doing, these aliens,
these Asians, Buddhists, Hindus, Muslims, Sikhs,
observing different holy days and weeks,
their women shrouded, following their men?
Strange gods they serve!

We're told to "love thy neighbour as thyself",
but who on earth invited these as neighbours —
their curry smells, their clothes, their strange behaviour?
Poor joke the Empire should reverse itself
and threaten our culture.

The peace of God which passes understanding
surpasses ours. Oppressed we go
back to our "Shangri-La", our bungalow,
out of sight of their terraced homes advancing;
has God forgotten who we are?

Roots

"I came from Gujarat," he said,
in his clean lace cap and beard.
"We came because the money was good,
it was hard, but we persevered.

"We had only one room for eight or nine,
we even shared the bed;
later we called our wives to come
as money and numbers spread.

"We were strangers in a foreign land
where no one understood
our faith and customs, or how we dressed,
and complained of the smell of our food.

"Your people have no fear of God,
drinking, eating pork;
your girls have forgotten their modesty —
shameless the way they walk.

"We planned to return when we earned enough,
we never planned to stay,
where cold winds blow through our terraced homes
and even the sun is grey.

"But our children enjoy the comforts you have,
they like it over here;
and some, like yours, have forgotten God —
why would they go back there?

"Yet still my heart is in Gujarat,
my dusty village and school,
the sugar-cane and buffalo
and after-sundown cool.

"I hear the cry of the village mosque
as here I join in namaaz,
while mother rests on her string charpai
beneath the changeless stars.

"Where is home? I've made it here
with children and my wife;
yet still I dream of all I left,
that hard but simpler life."

Bombay Mix

No cathedral this— a plain low hall
beside an abandoned church. But wall to wall
it's packed with eager worshippers, in jeans
or suits or saris, parents, children, teens,
Punjabi, Pakistani, Central Asian,
some British born, diverse and growing fusion
of east and west.
                The call to worship comes;
guitars and keyboard, drums, their rhythm thrums
to fill the little space. Bodies sway
hands raised, snatching silences to pray.
The Word is read and preached, the bread is
broken, thanks, notices and blessing spoken.

And once again our voices rise to fill
the room with noisy chatter, and we spill
into the kitchen. Spicy food completes
the celebration, with tea and Indian sweets.

We're learning love, and how the heart of God
wills to make us one, and why He trod
with such fixed purpose to a stake
to reconcile the world. The bread we break
is rich, but how much richer fare is planned
for billions more from every tongue and land;
what spices wait for those from sin released,
who've heard the invitation to his feast.

9/11

A clear dawn; the twin towers gleam.
Silver planes, precise as hawks, wing
clean to their target and rip at a country's seam
in blind hatred; its bitter fruit is falling —
squalls of glass, people, concrete, metal.
The city halts appalled, choked in the dust
of disbelief, while the world looks on and trembles;
man's hopes for peace are shattered in distrust.
Armies assemble, fleets set sail,
nations confer. In the mountains of a shattered land
a suspect hides, defiant. And all creation
grieves again as waves of anger expand.
Where are you God ? Why don't you restrain
the folly of mankind, take charge and reign?

War on Terror

How defeat terror? With terror?
Tragic error,
short memory!
A century
ago the war "to end all war"
bred hate and more
red virulence of violence.
Peace walks unarmed and suffers long,
like that man strong
we vilified
and crucified.

Crowns Imperial

Her majesty descends the stairs.
Magnificent the robes she wears,
concealing splendid powerlessness;
it was no frailty or fault of hers
that lost an empire.

A jewelled cross surmounts her crown,
that thing where pain and death abound,
where once the greatest king on earth
hung dying as the sun shut down,
rejected by his people.

Its scars now glorify the king
whose reign is hidden, though it brings
peace to a warring planet.
Knots on the cross of suffering
go with the grain of the world.

Christ stoops to rule, swings wide the doors
of heaven to undeserving poor,
washes their feet, calls them to serve
and follow as He goes before;
a cross surmounts their crowns.

Touching Simplicity

Let's not by claims to greatness be beguiled;
the Lord was once a baby at the breast
and calls us to him simply as a child.

When mothers brought their children, Jesus smiled;
He welcomed them with joy, and they were blessed;
let's not by claims to greatness be beguiled.

The Lord made friends with sinners, with reviled
and broken failures, chose them as his guests,
each came to him as simply as a child.

The Lord opposed conceited men, self-styled
as leaders and by vanity possessed;
let's not by claims to greatness be beguiled.

If with our God we would be reconciled
the way is faith in him who loves us best;
He calls us to him simply as a child.

Within the glorious Kingdom, undefiled,
the humble and the trusting find their rest;
let's not by claims to greatness be beguiled,
God calls us to him simply as a child.

Morning Invitation

Your Majesty, you've summoned me
and I am waiting, longing.
Hearing aids out, my ears are open,
your book on my lap.
Thanks that your planet's still on course
to let the sun through my window,
and for all it shows me —
dad's self-portrait frowning behind his glasses,
the fiery gladioli in their vase,
the photos of children and their children.
Thanks for the garden glimpsed outside,
the cut-glass sparkle of dew on the grass,
the feathery-purple acer
and early birds on the feeder.
Thanks Lord for the silence, good on my ear,
and for the faithful pumping of my heart.
Please now still my mind's debate
and draw me to your holiness.
I'm naked before you, there's nothing I can hide
in secret nooks or crannies of my life.
I trust in what you've done for me,
that you accept me as I am.
Please Lord speak,
for I long to hear.

Most Low God

My Lord, you are the strangest God,
You who dreamed the universe,
made matter out of nothing,
caused it to evolve and filled it
with teeming multitudes of lives.
You get on your knees to tend it,
hold microbes in your fingers,
delight in insects and worms,
care about the smallest bird
and the neighbour's stray cat.
O infinitely wise designer,
ever inventive artist,
patient and powerful,
most high, most holy,
inhabiting eternity,
yet most low God.
You get your hands dirty
washing dusty feet.
Your own feet bled once
nailed to a bit of wood.
My Lord, you are the strangest God;
you care even for me.

The Great Lover

All the workings of my brain
are known to You, my Master —
the words and phrases, symbols that I use,
my ignorant gropings.
You field my prayers with grace,
know the heart behind the stumbling,
a dad who understands his child.
Language gives out,
and when You're closest
I am silent
to rest my brain, myself,
in You.
For You are all,
my origins and ending,
centre and circumference,
and most true lover.

Grandson

His stillness surprised me. I had no need
to make strange sounds or jiggle him to soothe;
we sat as though our silence was agreed,
this man of just eight months, in whose smooth
gums there swelled a single tooth…and grey friend,
his grandad. Silently, alert, he gazed,
watching the world, trying to comprehend,
each fresh new object carefully appraised.
He had no words, and yet I seemed to sense
his infant spirit speaking unconstrained
by sentences, lucent in innocence
and full of trust, whom guilt had not yet shamed.
A tender loan from God, you challenge me
to learn from you, in fresh simplicity.

Colour Harmonies

Wearing blue-tank-engine-Thomas boots,
helmet blue and bigger than his head,
Zac whizzes wildly on his bike.

Unconscious of her crown of curling gold
Grace stomps in puddles, pushing a pink pram,
giving her dollies an erratic ride.

Jos, beneath a pure white shawl, lies still,
his wide and wondering eyes grasping to catch
meanings in a world just twelve weeks old.

Grey Gramps and Granny follow slowly,
delighted and fatigued by these young lives
so full of joy among the falling leaves.

Till Death us do Part

Proud horses yoked to a plough,
forty years kept in step,
more or less; tiring now.

Two ageing oysters side by side,
grit to each other's pearls, sharp
in gestation; Jeweller's pride.

Wine in cob-webbed bottles stored,
concealing silent processes,
waiting to be poured.

Speak up Please

No, I'm not Milton, grieving the loss
of one of his senses ere half his days were done.
I'm just an O.A.P. and ....what was that?
Yes, perhaps I'm getting deaf.

The birds no longer sing, excepting rooks;
sounds travel through fog. I seem to miss
signals in the crackle and hiss of my receivers.
Is this how it feels to be deaf?

Strange how the wife keeps mumbling, and people speak
so slovenly, and background music on the box
drowns conversation at the front.
Certainly I must be getting deaf.

I'm told the higher frequencies have gone —
my wife is filtered out, and gadgets in my ears
can't catch the music of her tones; it's hard
being close when one is deaf.

In press of crowds, when sounds swirl like the sea,
be patient with this old fool, and speak up please;
let him not retreat into the silence,
get too used to being deaf.

First Time

An undress rehearsal

The ticker's tired. After seventy years
can you expect to pass your MOT
without a spot of bother? Just a warning
intimation of mortality —
first time.

But what humiliation for a man
who thought himself still virile, this boring
diet of chemicals, and worry about
cholesterol or calls celestial
before my time.

Before my time. The NHS machine
struggles to defer the awkward moment,
yet even those who claim to live by faith
are tested when they glimpse the one-way gates
first time.

I wonder what lies beyond? Oblivion?
A Being unapproachable in splendour?
Or One who tasted what it feels like from
inside, who having died will hold my hand
next time?

In Hospital

No sun to gild the curtains;
a grey Manchester morning
peers through the windows, stirring
these derelict hulks.
I am a smouldering log
and an iceberg, by turns.
Shall I emerge alive?
Not much comfort to know
that others have walked this way before,
though they say an autumn bonfire
destroys pests,
and precious metal
is heated often in the fire.

Convalescence

Slowly the tide slides in
easing along my sides
forcing itself between the pebbles and my hull.
I hardly feel its lift-off
as I shift gently in shallow water.
And You are on board
skillfully fitting me out for the high seas.
You shall sail with me in my frail craft
Master most wise
Lord of the tides.

An Old Fool?

For Philip Larkin

Outwardly we are wasting away, yet inwardly we are being renewed day by day."

Yes, I think I must be on the way
to joining the old fools. My mouth as yet
doesn't hang open, but my hair is grey,
my memory leaks, and I need a hearing aid.
I've lost my energy; through heat or wet
one time I'd walk some fifteen miles and more
and climb high in the Lakes. I never made
much use of doctors then; now I know them well,
and what goes on in hospitals. I snore,
according to my wife, and tend to snooze
after the evening meal; truth to tell,
              I sleep half the News.

I can't ignore it, bits of me decay –
I'm getting old, the lights inside my head
show me, sometimes, happenings of yesterday
as vividly as if they happened now,
childhood on the farm, silly things I've said,
the rude shock of first days in the army.
On a pension I'm just one of a crowd,
a grey statistic. So is it now all
downhill – ash hair, toad hands, prune face, and barmy?
Breaking up? Thank God I'm not there yet;
there's still some time before the curtain falls
              on the final set.

59

Oh yes, I see extinction's alp stand clear
as days draw on and friends go on ahead.
But losing bits of me, the thing I fear,
means I travel lighter on the climb
and learn to depend upon a friend instead
of my own strength. I've set myself to live
for him who made these ranges; beyond time
He offers space for fools. And even now inside
our heads He shares the fading light, to give
hope to those crouching in shadow. The day
breaks when fools grow wise; they trust the guide —
who is himself the way

Percy's Pilgrimage

Percy was a clever boy
who did quite well at school;
they made him prefect his last year,
for Percy was no fool.

But some strange lack of confidence
sapped at his power to lead;
authority deserted him
in times of special need;

When discipline was called for
to curb some schoolboy fray,
too scared to be unpopular,
he looked the other way.

To national service he was called —
he tried for the Queen's commission
and soon became a subaltern;
he relished this position.

But all his swagger on parade
was like a thin veneer;
the army looked for leadership,
he fought an inner fear.

He failed to rouse the men one dawn —
"Stand-to" he should have cried.
The men slept on, the major fumed,
and Percy lied.

Two years of national service done
Percy went to college;
he wasn't sure what he should do,
except acquire some knowledge.

He'd always had some sense of God
and felt a calling dim
somehow to serve, but what that meant
quite eluded him.

He went to train for ministry,
learnt discipline and prayer,
but God seemed grim and distant still —
did He truly care?

The child in Percy cried inside
for love, acceptance, peace,
but Percy's God was strict and made
his sense of guilt increase.

A curate he became in time
in a grimy northern town;
he worked all day to get to God
and earn a holy crown.

He visited each afternoon
all those in special need,
and led all sorts of services
while doubting half the Creed.

He struggled when preparing talks,
they were a pain to hear;
on Saturdays before he spoke
he suffered from diarrhoea.

And then by chance he met a girl
whose faith was clear and strong,
who argued with him from St. Paul,
suggesting he was wrong.

He wondered who this woman was
to challenge all his doubt,
who threatened him with simple truths
he thought he knew about.

He went to see a Baptist friend —
a Baptist you may say?
A Church of England clergyman
leaving the narrow way?

His Baptist friend was very straight,
"Have you asked Jesus in?"
Percy replied , "He walks ahead —
I struggle with my sin."

They asked the Lord to enter then,
kneeling on the floor,.
and Percy began to feel quite new
as he opened wide his door.

He nearly cried, the tears welled up
for joy at his new-found life;
the woman rejoiced along with him,
and later became his wife.

They shared their struggles and joys together
serving the Lord they knew;
they stumbled and fell, but always found
their God to be totally true.

When Percy died his coffin displayed
an L plate, to proclaim
how Percy had always been eager to learn,
once God set his heart aflame.

They also gave him a "P" in green,
for Percy knew he had passed
by grace from the dark of his earlier years
into God's presence at last.

Downsizing

When extra beds lie empty
and sounds of children rare;
when doors are kept closed on the landing
and dust settles there;
when stairs feel so much steeper
that one has to pause for breath;
when the grass on the lawn grows longer
and the urge to mow grows less;
when the back stiffens quickly
bending to weed the borders —
then it's time to downsize.

It's hard after years in a place
to part with what's been cherished,
the Georgian-style sideboard
or the vast glass-fronted bookcase.
But there's no attic or cellar
for outsized stuff
in a two-bedroom flat.

Ah, but it's good
not to climb stairs
nor feel the extra draughts
which blow through a house of character.
No need to fret over unmown grass
or weeds in the borders.
With one foot on the bus-stop
we've a pass to go with it.
And still the children can come —
just long enough so we're not too tired,
and we can watch their progress.
Oh yes, there's much that's good
in downsizing.

Would that we could camp here
till we're carried out feet first —
but that's beyond our planning,
and one of us at least
may have to move again.
There's no lasting freehold;
we must all be downsized
when the final call comes,
before at at last we're welcomed,
trembling and surprised,
into the generous mansions
of our Father

Into the Light

For Dylan Thomas

Do not go faithless into that goodnight,
nor rage against the body's slow decay;
beyond the darkness shines his warmth and light.

Though sun and moon and stars may burn less bright
and glowing summer colours fade to grey,
do not go faithless into that goodnight.

Though family and friends pass on, despite
the things undone we meant to do and say,
beyond the darkness shines his warmth and light.

Though shameful memories and guilt invite
despair, a sense of failure or dismay,
do not go faithless into that goodnight;

however we have failed in what is right,
the righteous One is still the living way;
beyond the darkness shines his warmth and light

and we shall dance in rapture at the sight
of Him whose presence is eternal day.
Do not go faithless into that goodnight —
beyond the darkness shines his warmth and light.

Lightning Source UK Ltd.
Milton Keynes UK
UKOW03f1812170814

237052UK00003B/95/P